21st
Century
Junior
Library

Cicada

by Michael Shoulders

CHERRY LAKE PUBLISHING * ANN ARBOR, MICHIGAN

Published in the United States of America by Cherry Lake Publishing
Ann Arbor, Michigan
www.cherrylakepublishing.com

Content Adviser: The Entomological Foundation (www.entfdn.org)

Reading Adviser: Marla Conn, ReadAbility, Inc

Photo Credits: © GIRODJL/Shutterstock Images, cover, 10; © Kevin Wells Photography/Shutterstock Images, 4; © KOMUNews/Flickr Images, 6; © USDAgov/Flickr Images, 8; © Anne Fitten Glenn/Flickr Images, 12; © Mandy Creighton/Shutterstock Images, 14; © KPG_Payless/Shutterstock Images, 16; © Decha Thapanya/Shutterstock Images, 18; © Ryan M. Bolton/Shutterstock Images, 20

LIBRARY OF CONGRESS CATALOGING-IN-PUBLICATION DATA
Shoulders, Michael, author.
 Cicada / Michael Shoulders.
     pages cm.—(Creepy crawly critters)
 Includes index.
 ISBN 978-1-63362-589-1 (hardcover)—ISBN 978-1-63362-769-7 (pdf)—ISBN 978-1-63362-679-9 (pbk.)—ISBN 978-1-63362-859-5 (ebook)
 1. Cicadas—Juvenile literature. I. Title. II. Series: Creepy crawly critters.

 QL527.C5S56 2015
 595.7'52—dc23   2015001402

Cherry Lake Publishing would like to acknowledge the work of the Partnership for 21st Century Skills.
Please visit www.p21.org for more information.

Printed in the United States of America
Corporate Graphics

CONTENTS

5 Little Monsters

15 Is That a Skeleton?

17 Insect or Lawn Mower?

21 Not Music to My Ears

22 Glossary

23 Find Out More

24 Index

24 About the Author

Cicadas have thick bodies.

Little Monsters

Cicadas are thick insects that grow up to three inches (7.6 centimeters) long. Their large wings are often clear with dark **veins**. Their size might make them look scary, but these insects cannot sting and are not poisonous.

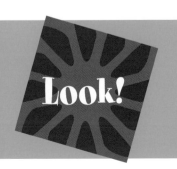

Look!

Cicadas actually have five eyes. The three smaller eyes form a triangle between the two larger ones. The little ones are called *ocelli*. That means "little eyes" in Latin.

These female cicadas are laying their eggs inside this tree branch.

A female cicada lays her eggs in the thin branches of trees. First she cuts tiny slits in the branch. Then she deposits her eggs with a special organ called an ovipositor. A few weeks later, **nymphs** hatch and drop to the ground. The nymphs are the size of ants. The nymphs dig between one and three feet (30.5 and 91.5 centimeters) into the ground.

These holes are from cicadas digging
themselves out of the ground.

The nymphs search for a tree root.
Their straw-like mouthparts are perfect for
piercing and sucking sap from the root.
They begin to grow. They spend most
of their lives hidden underground. Some
will not see daylight for many years.

Make a Guess!

Different types of cicadas spend different amounts of time underground. Some are there for only two years. Some are there much longer. Can you guess why?

The cicada leaves behind its
smaller skin as it grows.

When it's time, cicadas dig to the surface and climb the nearest tree. It is usually the same tree they've been feasting on for years. Then they go through their final **molt**, growing out of their older, smaller skin. They leave their old skin behind on the tree.

This cicada belongs to a 2008 brood in North Carolina.

Most cicadas live between two and five years, but some live much longer. They tend to come out of the ground in large groups called **broods**. Some broods remain buried up to 13 years. Other broods **emerge** after 17 years. It is a mystery how cicadas know it is time to come out of the ground.

These exoskeletons have been left on a tree trunk.

Is That a Skeleton?

Have you ever seen a six-legged shell on the side of a tree? If so, it's probably the shell, or **exoskeleton**, of a cicada. When it emerged, it slowly unfolded its wings and stretched out its **abdomen**.

Male cicadas make noise to attract females.

Insect or Lawn Mower?

The male cicada is one of the loudest insects on earth. He can be as loud as a lawn mower. His noisemaker, called a **tymbal**, is part of his body. He forces it back and forth so fast it sounds like a hum. If it were slower, it would sound like clicks. The humming sound attracts females.

Cicadas find their mates by making noises.

The female responds to the male with single clicks. It sounds exactly like fingers snapping. If you want to get a cicada to notice you, don't whistle. Simply snap your fingers. There is a good chance the male will come toward your hand. He will think it is a female.

Think!

What do you think would be the advantage to being the loudest cicada in an area?

This *Zammarra* cicada lives in
the Amazon rainforest.

Not Music to My Ears

Imagine a cicada brood emerging from the ground at the same time in a small area. The males all start singing to attract females. It gets pretty loud. For this reason, male cicada singing has been called one of the most annoying sounds on earth.

Ask Questions!

Most people who have heard cicadas never forget the sound. Ask a parent or grandparent if they remember hearing broods of cicadas. Ask them to describe the sound to you.

GLOSSARY

abdomen (AB-duh-muhn) the rear section of an insect's body

broods (BROODZ) groups of animals that hatch at the same time

emerge (i-MURJ) to come out from being hidden

exoskeleton (ek-so-SKEH-luh-tun) hard, protective covering

molt (MOHLT) to lose old skin so that new skin can grow

nymphs (NIMFS) a name used for some insects, including cicadas, that have not yet become adults

tymbal (TIM-buhl) a vibrating membrane in certain insects, such as the cicada

veins (VAYNZ) the stiff, narrow tubes that form the framework of a leaf or an insect's wing

FIND OUT MORE

BOOKS

Sutherland, Joshua and Chris McNab. *Social Insects*. New York: Gareth Stevens, 2007.

Amstutz, Lisa J. *Cicadas*. North Mankato, MN: Capstone Press, 2014.

WEB SITES

National Geographic Kids: Cicada

http://kids.nationalgeographic.com/animals/cicada/
Read some basic facts about cicadas.

How to Catch Cicadas

http://www.masscic.org/howto/how-to-catch-cicadas
With a parent, you can follow these detailed instructions to find and catch cicadas.

Origami Cicada Instructions

http://www.origami-instructions.com/origami-cicada.html
Follow these easy instructions to make your own origami cicada.

INDEX

A
abdomen, 15

B
body, 4
broods, 12, 13, 21

D
digging, 7, 8, 11

E
eggs, 6, 7
exoskeleton, 14, 15
eyes, 5

F
females, 6, 7, 16, 17, 19, 21

L
life cycle, 13

M
males, 16, 17, 19, 21
mating, 18
molting, 11

N
nymphs, 7, 9

O
ovipositor, 7

S
size, 5
skin, 10, 11
sounds, 16, 17, 19, 21

T
tymbal, 17

U
underground, 7, 8, 9, 13

W
wings, 5, 15

ABOUT THE AUTHOR

Michael Shoulders is a retired educator. When not writing, he travels the United States and Europe speaking to children at schools about the "magic of reading." He is a sought-after speaker at schools, for teacher in-service trainings, and at reading conferences.